Euphoria

A Collection of Glimmers

Written by
LiAna Maria Rivera

Dedicated to the optimists, the young-hearts, and the free spirits.

-AWAKENING-

Feather

Your soft delicate wisps of white,
Shielded me from scary sights,
Kept me alive through blinding light.
Fluttering through the soft blue sky
Fly away and know,
I truly don't mind.
For I shall keep
What you've left behind.

Beautiful September

Beautiful September is passionate.
When leaves start to crinkle,
And hot weather dies.
September; when my sign arrives;
It balances my mind.
September; a time when the moon is bright
September; a time I can bloom at night
As the wind breathes cool delight.
Beautiful September:
When the sunlight beams, but doesn't burn;
And the crows fly and the ravens sing,
In macabre, dark, circular rings.
Beautiful September; where I belong.
When the evening breeze lingers throughout the day.
Beautiful September is passionate.
A time when all my problems wither away.

Raven

When I hear the raven cry,
I hear my true name.
I catch a glimpse of the raven's wing
As she flies throughout the sky.
She sings beautiful songs of daytime
Even in eerie moonlight.
The raven perches herself at my side,
As I lay in a garden of roses alight.
Beneath the moon and the stars of night.
This raven is my soul's companion
My lovely little spirit guide.

Universe

Ravens screech with anger laced
throughout their tone.
Mumbling sweet hymns of death—breed
murder in the night,
The sky bleeds red while the moon is new.
It's darker than black, twinkling in the air
Quartz rain; tears drop from the moon of
darkness.
And the girl who dwells inside it.
She who controls the land.
This land is a land where hail is black and
burnt like coal;
A haven she calls her mind.
Every kiss received freezes the seas
All eyes locked and paralyzed in fright.
Black fire keeps the plants cool.
This girl and her tiny little pets, too.
Whole universes exist within her mind,
And she hasn't a clue.

Shivering sprinkles soar across the sky.

The seas sing tunes of the deep; sorrowful and blue.
Songs of the broken, weeping, and lone.
Shattered pieces of a porcelain doll:
Cracked skin, glassy eyes
Is all she can see shining through the light.

The girl who lurks inside the moon;
Confined alone to just one room.
Whole universes exist inside her
And she hasn't a clue.

Illuminated

Her eyes bleed diamonds;
Illuminated teardrops,
A trail on her cheeks
Against dusty moonlight.

The Abyss

Set the rose alight;
Let the smoke rise high into the air.
Let it carry her old life far in whirling wisps of white
Gleaming lights from burning petals shone bright;
It illuminated her dress with a thin flame of gold.
Igniting her inside-out;
A burning rose lit ablaze
As she danced alone;
Bleeding the past away.
Her moon beam burned through the red dusk.
Such big eyes drawn to a deeper essence—
An ethereal existence.
She reached into that bleak abyss,
And beyond it
She found salvation.

R e b i r t h

Dressed in pink ribbons and black laced lingerie,
Ink scrawled from her hand onto a coffee-stained page!
Her tears kissed the canvas;
Watercolor clear, but distorted.
Lonely in love are those who bear sorrow.
But when the light left her eyes,
A new moon rose,
Transparent against the blackened night.
Drizzles of rain-glow kissed her fingertips,
And with it she painted stars across the sky.

Roses in the River

I love the contradiction that is me.
A rose that blooms in the river.
I travel through the water,
A place called home across the river.
Into an ocean where many dangers wait,
But there's nothing that exists in this world
More dangerous than the past.
I ride the wave of my wildest dreams,
Following the call of my soul,
And sleep while the tides are calm.
Until I find myself adrift in a new river
Where great adventures wait for me.
I cross through mountains and valleys and plains.
A lone rose in the river of life.
I slowly find
Other roses like me
Blessed with grace and creativity.
In a place we should all be drowning
Is where we can truly be free.

Roses in the river of blank scenery,
The stars guide our way.
A canvas in our minds—the purest kind.
And the scents on our petals keep us alive.
As we roam together though dark and light,
Bearing nothing but our beautiful minds.

-INSPIRATION-

Key

Inspiration comes to me at the most inopportune times
But provides me a perfect outline
To create something bigger than myself.
Inspiration leaks through fat, wrinkled grooves in my brain,
So, I scribble down words and pictures to keep me sane.
I unleash waves, waves, and waves of creativity
And release mere drops of my insanity.
To make a beautiful work of art upon a blank canvas.
On white, blue lined sheets of paper,
Here is where I've discovered the key to happiness.

Stardust

I want to make an expedition into space...
No helmet or mask or oxygen tank.
To sleep in the waves of invisible dark matter,
And dream in grey creatures' company.
Wake up to the view of the Milky Way;
Bask in the coolness of limitless space
And kiss the moon with my fingertips.
Space is the only place I can truly be free,
To travel across this vast galaxy,
I want to run,
Forever lost,
In an endless river
Of scattered stardust.

Art–Form

My blood is ink
With hands of an artist,
Sawdust dances like visions in my dreams.
I sweat beads of watery clay.
My skin is pages, pages, and pages
Of parchment papers scorched with
Scribbles and doodles!
With each word, emotions unravel.
Beats of a song throb within my chest
And travels through my voice—
Can't you hear that music in the air?
My eyes are embers that flicker with light,
And my lips sparkle with kisses from the sky.
I am personified art in a mortal body,
With bits of my soul scattered across all galaxies.

Birth of Inspiration

A mind hidden in a thick haze of puffy grey.
Roses bloom across my psyche.
Petals flitter into my eyes through teardrops.
It paints a picture of meticulous design
Upon a cracking canvas of white.

Brain

I live in a city built in a sea
I float in a boat where I giggle with glee.
It's a city with grooves and winding roads
Where ideas grow and grow and grow!
This city in which I live that floats in a sea,
Of blood, grey matter, and electricity
It's a utopia for me!
This city in the sea is the haven of her mind.
Where she dreams, sees, and frees her eerie sublime.

Faeries

My tears crystallize in the light of a
thousand suns
And I drink the rain sprinkling
Through the evening breeze upon the
mountainside.
Illustrious lands of green and blue
We are faeries far, and few.

Cherry Blossoms

Cherry blossoms wither,
They fall and come back together.
In seas of pink, they roll with the waves.
At night on the beach,
On a riverside in the city
Or even in old country lakes.
Cherry blossoms bloom strong—
iridescent.
Pink and white then green, suddenly.
Their time with us— evanescent.
Words I found hidden in the psyche of my mind,
This newfound ink— effervescent.
Blood was spilled from my heart of glass,
No longer shattered from my past.
A light shining bright from deep within.
Cherry blossoms wither,
They fall and come back together.
Roll in the waves,
Kiss my cheeks,
Scatter to flurries

All around me.

Fire

A flame set alight
Blinding a person cloaked in gray.
Burn it away,
Burn it away,
Burn regret, hatred, and guilt away.
Light her up with a thousand flames,
Eyes gleam bright—
A reflection of herself.
The sun is brilliant,
The flames are bright.
A fire set alight inside
Fear does not exist here.
Even in the dark, her heart bleeds gold
This fiery light shines from her soul.

Air

Close your eyes.
Feel the wind against your skin,
Go on, love, breathe it in.

Hear your thoughts,
Spread your arms
Let them see your wings while it kisses
your cheeks.
Breathe it in slowly.

Cradled in its gentle arms
The sky is bathed in blush.
Gracing the space with clarity
The sun descends
As the golden aura burns into dusk.
Breathe it deep into your lungs.

It travels across the sky,
Far away from this mundane life.
It can carry your soul through the night.
Let go.

Don't fight.
Just turn off the light,
And breathe it in slowly.

Impossibility

I want a house and a garden by the water
That shines with glimmers of the sun.
I want a grand piano that plays on its own.
I want a house haunted by spirits of light
Where fae and shadows dance at night.
I want to fall in love,
I want to be alone.
I want to get married in the Palace of Versailles.
I want a family,
I want to make money,
But people say
"You can't have everything.
You should compromise,
Because you want too many things
That are *Impossibilities*."
So instead I'll settle for nothing less than my dreams.
Because it's all I can do:
Dream and dream and dream and dream

In this world of *Impossibility*.

Fly Away

They can't hold me down,
I will never stay.
These wings were made
To fly away.

Don't hold me too close,
I'll just run
And never turn back to you.

These wings have been stagnant
They ache in pain.
I can't take this anymore.,
I must find a way.

Alone in the air as I soar through the sky
They can't shoot me down with their evil eyes.
Go ahead and try,
Give me a reason to cry.
I dare you all to tear me apart.

It doesn't matter what you say with your weak little mind,
Because my dreams are stronger than you.
These words pump blood through my beating heart,
All my pain transforms into art.
But go ahead
And make me cry
Because my dreams,
My drive,
The tears swimming in my great big eyes,
And these beautiful black wings
Are mine.

I'm not sorry to say,
That I must fly away;
You can't hold me back anymore.
These wings inside me are aching in pain.
I must find a different way.
The will of my heart is stronger than ever
I am all I need.
These dreams of mine
They'll learn to fly

I just need to spread my wings.

You can't hold me down
I will never stay.
These wings were made
To fly away.

Head In The Clouds

Innocent eyes gleaming
Curiosity peeking
Through chocolate-sweet irises.
Wandering thoughts
Exist within her mind
Bring her clarity,
Like a crisp autumn breeze.
Whistling wind across the sky.
"Her heads in the clouds."
They all say,
"She dreams of a life too far away."
She'll humor them with a smile,
Then raise them a riddle,
"If my dreams exist too far away,
And I'm clouded in mind
From my head to my toes;
If these dreams can't exist in this reality,
Then why do they feel so close?"

-SELF LOVE-

Closed Curtains

Soft, velvet fabric
Rich color—bleak.
Cold from brisk air
Sun-dust rising with the wind,
Blowing in.
To open them would beckon the light
But I prefer to keep them drawn shut.
Within the darkness of this empty house,
I have found solace
In solitude.

The Empress

My mind is fertile ground where flowers bloom.
The words ascend through the scents in the air.
I can feel the rain wash over me,
Leaving dewdrops behind on my petals.
I can twirl the stems between my fingers and smile.
I can feed on the energy alive around me,
Expanding my mind with beautiful words.
The prose: quaint little pieces of me,
The song of my heart is poetry.
I am the empress,
Fertile with the words
My body holds within.
I am mother to all these creations you see,
Such a beautiful life I live.

Self Care

Laces down her back and cheeks flush
with color
Sunset streams through the curtains,
Bathing the room in pink.
White candles lit and slivers of smoke kiss
the air.
The scents entice her soul
And she can breathe in the sweet air of
ecstasy.

Release onto satin upon a bed of blooming
roses.
She can bend and twist and curl her toes
And her mind is filled with colors.
Her body shakes and her lashes flutter
Happy tears roll from beneath.
Her heart beats
A rhythm fills her ears like music sheets.
Her hand is cramped as she lifts it away,
Limp beside her.

She faces away from the streaming light;
The wind blows out the candles.
She smiles and lies her head on a pillow,
Slipping into a dream.
Unapologetically she can love anyone,
Yet needs none but herself.

Spanish Rose

One night I fell asleep
In a garden of red roses.
The moon kissed my cheeks,
And the rain cleaned my face.
The next morning
As the sunrise shone down on me,
The wind whisked me away.

Life

I'd rather live a life of vague delusion
Than one of painful regret.
I'd rather chase after dreams and stars
Than little babies from a man that only
serves to depress.
If that means I may die old and alone with
a cat,
I'll take that death a thousand times over.
This life you call one of delusion is the
happiest life I could live.
Because my heart, my soul, my mind, my
dreams,
They all belong to me.
And all these visions I see
Are the meaning of life for me.

Shy Girl

She was a shy girl
Who sipped sweet honeysuckle
And toxic milk from plumerias
As they scattered across the schoolyard.

Monarch Butterfly

I will be your monarch butterfly
My eyes reflect the light of the sun
Transformed into a beautiful dream.

Rose Gold Eyes

A girl was born of dark hair and sunshine.
She believed in love and all that was kind.
The sweetness of honeysuckle dripped
from her tongue.
Her eyes gleamed with paint of golden
tears
The waves; an endless stream of riches.
She has rose-gold eyes of innocence
In them she sees everything through a
filter of light,
Everything is beautiful in her eyes; and
everyone is good.
Her heart feels that of a rose-gold love
And it never leads her astray.
This girl who was born of dark hair and
sunshine
Sees light in every life.
Through her beautiful rose-gold eyes.

Sugar Skull

My sugar skull love speaks to me
In sweet tongues of epiphany.
Her eyes framed with fuchsia pink petals,
The twinkle in her eye reflect diamonds in the air
And her tears are glitter,
Speckled everywhere!
She sings to me through her teeth
Sweet songs of infinity.
That speak of self-love and inward divinity.
With rose-colored irises, she beams down on me.
Swirled designs rest on her cheeks of filigree
Her face gently painted calligraphy.
When she speaks to me, she sings!
Sweet songs of us, and songs of we
Because I am "we" and she is "me",
My sugar skull love, indefinitely.

Self-Portrait

I draw on my legs through rips in my
jeans.
I can't help it sometimes,
Because you see,
I'm simply surrounded by things
That inspire me.
Long lashes and wavy wisps of hair
Flow across my face,
Down to my knees.
As I sit in this meadow of clarity
While my own self-portrait stares back at
me.
She has my eyes,
My laugh,
My cry.
The doodles I draw
Across my thigh
Are pieces of me
In every light.

A Love Letter to Me

I love her, for she is me.
Raven black hair,
And eyes sweet like honey.
I see footprints on a sandy beach
I will follow along the path she leaves.
I hear her voice calling to me.
I will chase after it until we meet.
I love her, for she is me.
There is no love truer
Than the love she dreams.
This love is unconditional,
Some may say *impossible.*
But either way
I love her, for she is me.
She sings sweet songs
She dreams big dreams.
Flowers bloom from her hair
In the braids she weaves.
Her skin smooth as silk
Her lips plump and pink
Sparkling like fizzy rosé in a glass.

Her voice makes wind
Echo through chandeliers of the sky.
Delicate, airy, tender and strong.
I love her, for she is me.
A girl who sings and writes poetry.
A girl who dreams, never asleep.
A girl who perceives what no one else can see.
A girl who breathes
A girl who's free.
I love her, for she is me.
And I love her unconditionally.

- DIVINE LOVE -

My Love Shrouded in Darkness

The darkness held me
In the absence of man.
The darkness kissed the salty tears on my face
Enveloped me in its warmth.
A warmth as furthest from human as it could get.
The darkness fills my heart to the brim with love;
A love once lost to me
The darkness whispers sweet nothings at night,
And loves to occupy my time.
Its paradoxical;
Impossible, simultaneously dark and light.
It loves me now and holds me tight.
In its eyes I see stars only visible at night;
That glimmer, and twinkle, and shine so bright.

My love shrouded in darkness with stars for eyes
Is all I want with me tonight.

The Little Things

What really matters to me are little things
The taste of hot cocoa against my lips,
The sound of a keyboard typing away,
Pencil sketches littered across the page,
The feeling of the wind against my face.
These words I write come effortlessly
The art I create just for me.
The songs I sing inspire me
I'm so amazed by the little things.
Ravens cawing, waking me
The sun shining and the rain falling.
Clouds drifting across our sky
Trees that fill us all with life.
The waves that roll across the sea;
The scent of saltwater in the breeze.
The life I have, I live perfectly.
If all that truly mattered in life was money,
Why are the blessed rich so… unhappy?
Happiness isn't as simple as materiality
I'm rich in life, freedom, and creativity.

So rich in things that cannot be seen
I take care of me and my little kitty.
I'll take care of my divine love
Once he finds me.
Everything made up of little things
That's what truly matters to me.
This vision of a life I see in my head,
If I can't have that,
I'd rather be dead.

Violets and Black Lace

A little girl dances in purple hues
Puffy clouds sprinkle rain that kiss flushed cheeks
And the beaming sun beats against her back.
She's clothed in black lace,
A beauty delighted
With violets in her hand and flowers in her hair,
She dances alone in the sun shining bright.
And she sits by a creek and tears a page from a book.
The page is engulfed in the watery streams
As it withers away into nothing.
The girl with violets and black lace
Mascara eyes of innocent bloom
And a subtle smile graces her face.
She dances in circles on her way back home

Where she sets the fresh-picked violets in a tall glass vase
And a book upon her Mother's bedside.
With a kiss on her forehead, she holds back tears
And places a violet in her fragile hand.

Adoration

Ever so happy he seems
As the brightest
Light in his eyes stare achingly from the deepest haze—
Such strong intensity reflected in his gaze.
Me, jaded in love,
Until I discovered the one whom I'd hold the strongest
Admiration, affection, and unrequited devotion…
He holds in his hands the hearts of many,
Yet never knowing me,
Who wrote this solely for him to read.
One day soon maybe he shall see,
One day soon maybe we shall meet,
But until then I shall
Dream, dream, and dream endlessly
For such a far-fetched fantasy.

Constellations

Pastel colors blend like dusty chalk across the stars;
High away from Earth in the deepest space.
Inside looming darkness hides,
But with you, light fills this perpetual night
And leads me straight to paradise,
Hypnotic eyes lure me into a dance
Lasting forever in stardust's time,
Illuminating the darkest recesses of our universe.
And now every constellation I see in the sky
Reminds me of your soft twinkling eyes.

Aiming High

I have been down this familiar road.
So many times before.
I touched this line of impossibility once.
But I believe I could go further.
When I dream of him, I feel I could do better.
When I dream of them, I want to aim higher.
And I shall continue this long, drawn out journey.
In an attempt to feel you close to me.

Beat

Once I'm in love, I never give up.
It's a curse, yet such a blessing.
My heart renews every time she breaks.
Each beat makes her stronger.

I'm in love with the way
He crinkles his nose;
He's witty, he's crazy;
He looks kind of funny;
I'm in love with his eyes,
His laugh, his face—
Damn it all, he drives me insane!
He provides me a purpose,
He keeps me strong.
I find solace in his voice,
Soft like a whisper.
The truth he speaks to me
Rages louder than heat in summer.
I can feel his heart beating
From miles away.
His smile warm like the sun,

Dark brown eyes; simultaneously mystic,
Euphoric, melancholic,
Perhaps even manic!
This man remains unrivaled in my heart.
He is my strength.
His words my rock.
He taught me how to fall in love;
And now I'm helplessly, hopelessly,
Addicted, it seems.

Once I'm in love, I never give up.
It's a curse, but such a blessing.
My heart will break
Over and over, so let her.
My heart replenishes every time she breaks,
And from this day, it'll beat for me;
The one whose love
Is everlasting.

Euphoria

Silken kisses flow through my heart,
Glimmering and scattered across the air.
I'm enveloped in his light.
I want nothing else.
His dark eyes are my shelter;
His outstretched arms are my home;
His beating heart against mine.
What we have isn't so simple as that word called love,
Rather something pure, something true, something real.
His chocolate dreamy eyes and lovely voice
Bring a feeling to me
I've only felt in my sweet, sweet dreams.
As he beckons me back into his embrace,
That strong façade of mine dies in his hands.
The sun crosses into my sight
And I know
He is Euphoria.

Ride All Night

On the back of your bike,
I could ride all night
With the wind in my hair
And the moon shining bright.

We'd pass highways, diners, tattoo shops,
Racing for miles on scorching asphalt.
The rays blare bright,
Reflect on the bike.
As sunspots nearly render me blind.
The engine's hum kisses our legs
And fills us both with energy.
We reach the dry countryside.
"No destination," you say.
"Let's just ride."
Your voice carries through the wind,
Scratchy and rugged from the desert air,
But I can still hear you so, so, so clear.
"Be careful, honey." and, "Hold on tight."
You tell me not to close my eyes.

Across the landscape past the mountains,
Abundant colors blend across the sky.
Orange, pink, purple, blue;
As black gradually bleeds through.
We're alone on the road; you and I.
Headlights and the moon; shining bright.
I rest my chin on your broad leather shoulder
To see a long infinite road.
You chuckle a sweet chuckle;
No words to follow,
And take me wherever you'll go.

On the back of your bike,
I could ride all night.
The wind tangles my hair;
Your eyes are the sky.

Fabric Flower Heart
Part II: Lotus

Peel away the layers of my fabric flower heart.
Touch each petal with your fingertips,
Light, airy, let them fly across that great blue sky.
And all along I wonder to myself,
"How can your love reach me from so far away?"
Peel back the layers of my fabric flower heart.
Taste each one between your lips,
Only to find me hiding inside.
Cradle my lotus flower in your hands,
You nurture me with your tender love
Kissing each paper-thin petal.
You place me gently upon the water
And watch me float across the great expanse of your love.
I am only safe in your arms.

You've peeled away my fabric flower heart,
You see me in all that I am.
A lotus blooming through the mud,
No one else could perceive that such a thing exists.
Who I truly am,
Love in the form of lilies abloom,
You who saw the beauty in me.
Both of us free to fly across that sherbet sky,
Yet never stray apart.
You and I,
Lotus flowers that only bloom
In the light of the moon and stars.

Crystalline Love

The love I feel for him is a crystal love—
Clear, brilliant and shining with light
from above.
I love the snow-drops I see in his eyes
That twinkle with the same glow
As those periwinkle skies.
I love the crinkles in the corners of his
eyes
His soft hair that curls like waves in the
wind.
I'm oh so deeply in love with him,
Dear me!
Through eyes like crystals I see.
This crystalline love that brews ever deep
Though he may never even catch a
glimpse of me.

With You

When I'm with you
The sky is bluer,
The birds sing louder;
The stars shine brighter;
The wind feels softer.
Summer is cooler,
Winter is warmer,
Spring is lighter,
And Fall is cozier.
Our heart beats faster,
Yet time goes slower,
Spent alone with you.

Lovers

Hold me tight,
Kiss me goodnight.
And when I wake up,
Shower me in roses,
Play with my hair;
That way I'll know
You'll still be there.

Forehead Kisses

When you kiss her like that
Roses sprout from her cheeks,
And goosebumps bloom across her skin.

Sun Kissed

He feels so warm,
His big arms are a home like I've never known.
Tan skin, bright eyes,
A smile that brings my soul to life.
I'm touched by his warmth
The sun on my skin
Kisses me softly
A glow from within
Forever shining down on me.
In this golden hour of night, he brings,
A flame burns ever bright.
He shines into my heart
With his glorious light.

Surrender

Kiss all the pain away from me.
Breathe your air into me.
Keep me grounded against you.
Bathe me blissfully in your water.
Protect me, my heart and soul.
Touch the invisible wounds inside.
Gaze at me with beaming eyes,
And a smile sweeter than honey.
Pull me close,
No reason to fight.
So, I'll let go of the pain
I'll leave it behind.
I'll release my body, heart, soul, and mind.
Surrender everything to this love.

Summer Blush

Silky waves move against my legs
Until I feel like I'm floating away.
Your hair dances in the wind;
Pink petals fly into it.
They cling to the water in your locks,
So, I float to you and pull them off.
Your eyes are soft like a twilit sky.
And your smile is warm like a kiss from the sun.
Oh, how nice an embrace would be
Amidst the light of these blossoming trees.
Even when the moon ascends,
The sun in your eyes is ever present.
Our stars aligned to make flowers bloom in spring.
The pink petals in our hair proves it so, my love.
And when the cold breeze of the moon drifts on by,
Keep me warm in your arms tonight.

When the wind tickles my nose,

You kiss my flushed cheeks

Locked in your gaze,

I can barely breathe.

But I'll survive if you hold me tight.

Our hearts beat as one and it feels so right.

Now because of you,

I don't hate spring as much.

Now because of you,

I love the sun,

And I've grown fond of my summer blush.

Because of you,

I've fallen in love.

Twin Flame

Even the heaviest rain
Cannot put out the flames
I have burning in my heart
For you.

Sanctuary

Sanctuary exists
Between you and me.
Sanctuary exists
In the world I see.
Of all the beautiful realities
Playing right in front of me,
I will choose
The one with you
From now
Until eternity.

Don't Say : "사랑해."

I won't say: "사랑해."

Until I do.
I won't ever say I need you
Because it won't ever be true.
I won't make any promises
That I can't keep to you.
So please

Don't say: "사랑해."

Until you feel it too.

My Love

My love for him is stronger than it once
was for them.
He never tries to hurt me the way they
used to.
He sees only me,
I am the apple of his eye.
I am the wine in his glass.
I am the one he thinks about all through
the night.
I am the only one who occupies his time.
His love for me is stronger than theirs
ever could be
His big arms protect me,
While he holds me in my sleep.
Cocooned in his warmth,
I feel most free
Because only with him I can truly be.
So, to all of them, I say
"Stop calling."
"Stop trying."
"Stop writing to me."

"Just give it up completely."
Because the one I love,
The only one for whom my heart beats,
His heart beats only for me.

Flustered

You fluster me, confuse me so
So much so, it's impossible!
You planted seeds inside my head
That grew into wildflowers.
Before I never used to care too much
About you
Or anything you do.
I took your voice for granted,
But now I hold on to every word you say
And to be honest, I can't fucking stand it!

Mask Part II: The Other Side

I want to fall in love with you
With all the parts you have.
Everything you've shown to me
And everything you mask.
I want to give you
Unconditional, unwavering, unrelenting
love.
So let me,
Don't reject me.
Please,
Don't leave me in the dusk.
Let me hold you and comfort you.
Let me be the one.

Dreams

The dreams I have aren't mindless desire.
I just want to be closer to you.
Let down your guard and let me in,
Let me love you for all that you are.
Share with me the shards
Of your quaint beating heart.
And I too, will share mine.
With two wholes of ourselves
We can make something beautiful
Just give me a bit of your time.

In Your Arms

In your arms, I am me:
Happy, funny, in love eternally.
In your arms, I can breathe.
Deeply, heavily, constantly.
In your arms, I am free:
Irreversibly, completely, indefinitely.
In your arms, I can see:
Clearly, ever so perfectly.
In your arms I can believe
In anything.

Our Time

The glittering sun shines against the water
Just like the twinkle alive in your eyes.
Your smiling bright eyes light up the sky
In them I see our future is bright.
I once floated alone in an ocean of fright.
Waves crashed across my body
Lost in the current,
But somehow, I made it out alive;
Spouted out from the ground,
A rose reborn.

Like a dove I fly
With you by my side
And every single day, I realize
That we live such a beautiful life.
To all past loves:
I've mourned,
I've cried,
And left all of them behind.
Because the light I see

Reflecting at me
Through your big brown eyes,
The light that shines so bright is mine.
Our future, our home, our paradise
Now it's our time.

Sweet

Lips shaped like hearts
A smile pure like a blanket of snow.
Eyes that shine like molten chocolate cake,
His laugh banishes all despair from me.
He's gentle, yet strong.
He's held me all along.
He loves me more than anyone.
He touches my cheeks
With candy sweet kisses.
He's my favorite,
Ever so sweet to me.

Sky

When I look at you,
I find myself
Gazing up at the sky.
Whether dark at night
Or bathed in light
I find myself
Lost in your eyes.
Eyes that beam like stars
Shining down on me
In my darkest hours.
The crescent moons of your eyes
Make them twinkle at night.
My teddy that holds me ever so tight.
You're warm and strong,
You are my sun.
No.
The sun by itself is too dim for your light.
To me, you're the entire sky.

Golden Love

Fill the cracks in my heart with our
golden love.
The essence of you brought me new life,
Both of us reborn
Into something more beautiful than ever
before.
Spill your gold straight into me,
Bless me with your masterpiece.
This mystical feeling inside of me,
I will let it flow through my veins.
With something more than a simple kiss,
Something deeper than love itself,
You've become part of me.
A rose has bloomed
Inside my womb
As I hear your voice calling for me.
When all is said and all is done,
You are my one, my one, my one.
I'll hold you tight,
And kiss you goodnight,
Goodnight, my golden love.

영원히

Yours Truly,

영원히

Forever,
I will be.

Kiss From a Raven

Roses and wine
My sweet valentine
Falling asleep to the sound of his song,
I know he'll never do me wrong.

I close my eyes and see his smile
Charming, iridescent, soft, and wild.
In these dreams,
I can see every star in the sky.
Petals scattering all around me,
Bathed in soft ecstasy.

Roses and wine
My sweet valentine
Falling asleep to the sound of his song,
I know he'll never do me wrong.

Silken sheets beneath me
Coax me to sleep.
From far away he holds me,
His words speak the melody of his heart.

Alone I lay
Yet I feel him close.
As if he's breathing right beside me.

Roses and wine
My sweet valentine
Falling asleep to the sound of his song,
I know he'll never do me wrong.

When I hear his voice,
Euphoric bliss radiates from my body.
Soft, gentle, like feathers flowing through the wind.
This earth angel cares for me from afar
A kiss from a raven soars across the sea,
As I close my eyes and fall asleep.

Roses and wine
My sweet valentine
Falling asleep to the sound of his song,
He will never do me wrong.

Blooming

I'm a little red bud sprouting
In your garden of crying violets.
Musical notes fall like rain from the clouds,
Nurturing my fragile state of mind.
Though we're at a great distance now,
You still find a way to lend me strength
To survive through every lonely night.
Thank you for shining that beautiful light.

I'm a lonely little bud spouting
In your garden of smiling violets.
Blooming slowly with every note you sing
These shy petals of mine
Unfold in the light of your smile.
You fill me with warmth,
Despite the rolling thunder shaking the sky
Rumbling across our fertile ground.
But you never fail to remind me,
Nothing in this world can tear us down.

When I hear your voice,
It moves me to tears.
Sadness, joy, elation,
And other emotions I've yet to experience.
Until I sprout through a crack in the cement
Inside your garden of crying violets.
Blooming alone;
Slowly, ever unfolding,
Poetry hidden in these layers of me
Hearing a song that sounds so sweet.
Coaxing me out of my shell.
You're a diamond that shines
In that midnight sky
Like dewdrops on petals
Fresh after rain.

A lone little rose
In your garden of smiling violets
How I love you so.
A soft little rose
In your garden of crying violets

Beaming up at a brilliant star,
Always dreaming of you.

If I keep growing,
Unfolding,
And molding
Into the best version of me
Will I too shine as bright as you?
Though even if I never do,
I know at least that I will bloom
In this glimmering, shimmering
Ethereal dream.
Seeing it all through your lens instead,
This beautiful world is the perfect gift.
The sempiternal spring—
Of you and me.

Bunny Bear

When I was a child,
My grandfather gave me
A stuffed rabbit,
One named Bunny.
But one night
I lost it.
While traveling across the country.
Time passed,
I forgot about Bunny.
Except at night
When I was so lonely.
See…
Bunny used to protect me
From the boogeyman and wild wraiths.
But when I lost it,
I became so sad
And the boogeyman appeared to me
With different faces,
Again and again and again.
I still remember my Bunny sometimes
It's big doe eyes,

Tan colored fur
And of course,
It's adorable teeth.
It's been too long
Since I've seen my Bunny.
Oh, how I miss it so.

Then as an adult
As if by some miracle
I hear an exciting laugh.
It pulls my ear, as I lift my head
To see a man
Taller than me.
He claps his hands,
Hops like a rabbit,
White teeth shining
His eyes closed in delight

And when that man saw me and stared
With the biggest eyes I've ever seen,
Euphoric bliss touched me
And just like that,
All memories of Bunny returned;

My childlike wonder,
Innocence rediscovered
As if by some miracle!
All these years, I thought I lost him
My stuffed rabbit named Bunny.
But the moment our eyes locked,
That's when I knew…
I knew I found him again.
I realized then
That the boogeyman
Was a figment of my imagination.

And now we sleep in a big comfy bed
Cuddling throughout the night.
A warmth in my tummy
Now that I've found my Bunny
Though nowadays,
He's bigger than me.

When it's cold,
He holds me close
Pressing kisses across my nape,
He plays with my curls

And inhales my scent
Coconut sweet just like him.
His healing aura envelops me,
Calling me to sleep,
In a dream of mermaids and butterflies;
Of apples and cherries
Of waterfalls and wildflowers
Of sunshine and rainbows
Sleeping safe like a child again.
And ever since I found my Bunny,
My life became so sweet.

Crescent Moons

When he smiles, his eyes shine
Like crescent moons.
How dark brown could beam so bright,
I never knew.
When I look into his eyes,
I can see the sky.
My lover shrouded in darkness:
Murky, mysterious, ambiguous in the night,
Disappeared the moment I saw you.
My lover shrouded in darkness with stars for eyes
Disappeared the moment I saw you.
Was it that he no longer loved me?
Or does my lover shrouded in darkness have a face now?
That now that I've seen him,
I can't unsee him.
You haven't left my mind since that moment.
I've never forgotten your name

Since I first heard it.
And I'm terrible with names,
I remember faces more;
I'm artistic, visual!
If you tell me to remember a name, a time,
a date, a place,
I won't, it's just not me—
Then how on earth did I remember
Your name?
Tell me, answer me please…
Was he you all along?
The man who's eyes shine
Like crescent moons
When he smiles like that at me?
The man who's deep dark eyes
Hold entire galaxies?
Too many similarities,
Some kind of familiarity,
But I can't place it.
Too many things I once thought
coincidence
And once you told me that it's not,
They began to stack up!

All these signs, synchronicities;
All these visions; all these dreams
I keep seeing you in them,
It's always you,
You never leave me be.
But I don't want you to.
No.
I want you to stay.
Occupy this space with me
Let everyone else think I'm crazy.
Though they're all just reflections of me,
The parts of me that believe
I don't deserve good things.
But even if we never meet,
Even if we only live our love in fantasy,
I'd rather gaze into your deep dark eyes
all damn night
Than never know brown could beam so
bright.
Your crescent moons,
Keep smiling at me.
Your crescent moons,
Keep shining at me.

Don't ever let me go,
And I'll hold you close.
Just stay here right beside me.

Home

Though there's a cloud hanging over my head tonight,
I can still see the glow of the moon.
Though a cloud hangs over my head tonight,
The thunder lights up the sky.

The rain can fall all around me tonight,
I will remain in silence.
The pitter-patter against a lonely street
Becomes a whispering melody.

My hair curls up
And my clothes turn cold
As the rain purifies me.
I open a book of poetry
One quite melancholy.
As tears from the clouds
Make the ink bleed,
I can see the pages so clearly.

Until a shadow of a man approaches me,
Holding an umbrella over my long wet curls.
His warm smile sparks a flutter in me
That I simply cannot resist
He holds his hand out to me,
Offering his heart
To become a shelter from the storm
raging in mine.
I take his hand and walk with him
And the rain follows close behind.

Though the clouds hang over our heads tonight
And the freezing rain surrounds us both
The warmth of our love
Lights our way back home.

Though the clouds beckon a dark night
And the thunder begs us to stay.
I know that he will keep me safe
Because I found home
In his embrace.

Glossary

사랑해: *I love you*

In Hangul (Korean Written Language)
Romanized: (sa-rang-hae)

영원히: *Forever*

In Hangul (Korean Written Language)
Romanized: (yeong-won-hi)

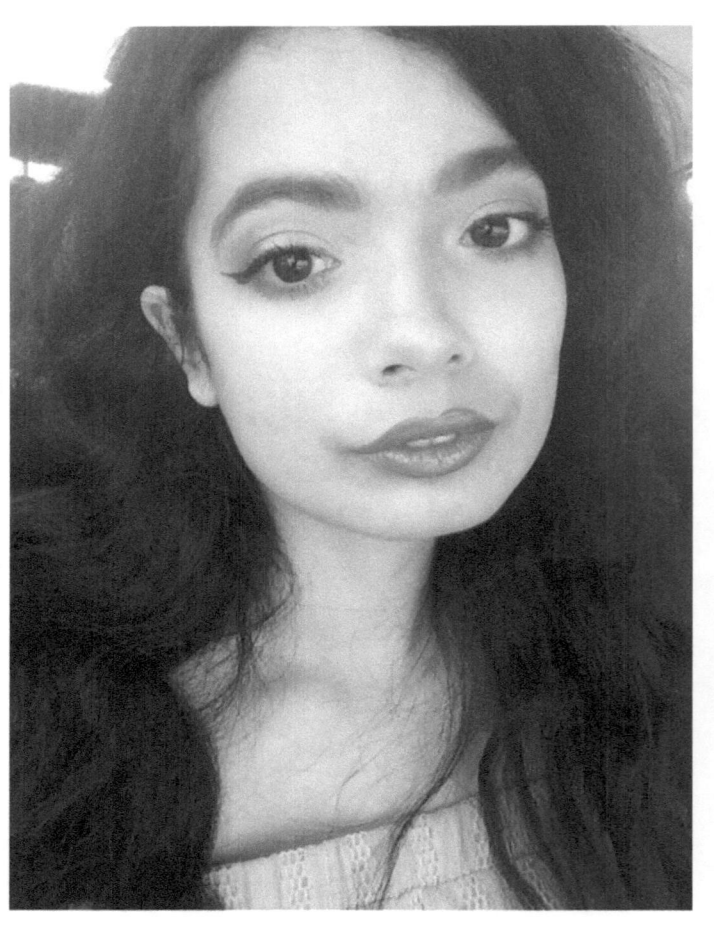

About the Author:

LiAna Maria Rivera is an artist of various mediums namely: writing, drawing, and music.
Her purpose in life is to call the inner melancholy that lay dormant within her and transform it into something beautiful in any creative way her mind wills it.
Her writing and art styles are heavily inspired by the romantic era of art and literature. As expected, she loves writing poetry, horror, and psychological thrillers. Despite this, she's a softie for beautiful love stories and likes to incorporate themes of love into a vast majority of her work.
She loves animals, but no animal more than Mr. BooBooKitty Cuddles, a black and white eight year young cat. Rainy, cloudy days spent cuddling with him and getting lost in a book are what happy times are made of for this strange lady.

When she's not cooing over how adorable her cat is, she's probably writing a blog post about how the decomposition process makes flowers shine brighter than the Supermoon.

Read *Euphoria: A Graphic Storytelling* for free on Webtoon!

Euphoria: A Collection of Glimmers
copyright © 2020 by LiAna Maria Rivera.
No part of this book may be used or
reproduced in any manner without
written permission except in the case of
reprints in the context of reviews.

ISBN: 978-1-951417-06-2

Cover Design and Illustrations by LiAna
Maria Rivera

www.ingramcontent.com/pod-product-compliance
Lightning Source LLC
Chambersburg PA
CBHW030335100526
44592CB00010B/705